AF225139

THE TRUTH

PLEZE RAYBON

"TRUTHFUL LIPS ENDURE FOREVER BUT A LYING TONGUE LASTS ONLY A MOMENT."

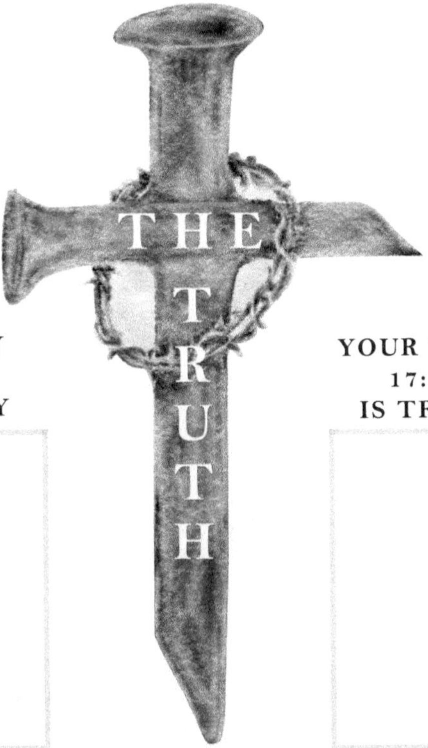

-PROVERBS 12:19

ReadersMagnet, LLC

CONTENTS

ACKNOWLEDGMENT

I thank God for the prayers of my two brothers: Rev. Fred Mcgirt and John Raybon. My two sisters: Joyce and Helen Raybon. My two beautiful children: Melea and Jesse Raybon I love, love, love you both!

INTRODUCTION

Acts 17:11

These Berea's were more noble than those in Thessalonica in that they received the word with all readiness of mind, and searched the scriptures daily.

It would be beneficial if we the people of God had that same attitude. There are a lot of different things being said, and many different teachings.

I understand that we have different revelations and insights, but some of these insights and revelations can be very misleading. There are many insights and revelations: but only one absolute truth! There are many questionable opinions: but only one absolute fact! So I have learned to study to show myself approved unto God, because therein lies the absolute truth.

So according to the truth: I can refute some of these teachings that are very misleading.

THE GAP THEORY

There are some who teaches that there was a thousand year gap in Genesis chapter 1 between verses 1&2. They claim: this is the result of Satan being cast out of heaven causing total chaos, utter confusion and disorder. These teachers agree that God created heaven and earth, and it was destroyed because of Satan's fall. This one minister said God doesn't create anything void and how can he create darkness if there's no darkness in him. They didn't stop there, they use one more scripture to try and prove a point. Genesis 1:28 where God blessed them and said be fruitful and multiply and replenish the earth and subdue it. I guess they were confused by the word replenish, because they are saying it means to refill.

Let's see what the truth has to say about all of that!

God the father created heaven and earth, and they are right on this one issue, He doesn't make any void: is it so hard to believe it was dark because God hadn't spoken the sun, moon and stars into existence and it was void or empty because God hadn't put anything on it yet? The term replenish: If you look at the Hebrew definition, you will find the word (maw-law) it means to fill or be full of. Maybe that is too simple for some.

The truth says in Exodus 20:11 for in six days the Lord made heaven and earth, the sea and all that in them is, and rested on the seventh day. If you really look closely at verses 1&2 of Genesis chapter 1 you will see the trinity at work.

God the Father created heaven and earth: How did he do it? With words! Who is the word? Jesus!

Listen to the truth of scripture. Eph.3:9 and to make all men see what is the fellowship of the mystery which was from the beginning of the world has been hid in God, who <u>created</u> all things by <u>Jesus</u> <u>Christ</u>.

Col.1:16 for by Him (Jesus) were all things created, that are in heaven, and that are in earth, visible and invisible whether they be thrones, or dominions or principalities, or powers, all things were created by Him and for him.

Before we go any farther I want to show you one key word that blows that teaching away, That key word is "And". We know that the word and is a continuation of a phrase: It's used three times in that verse, the last one being key <u>And the Spirit of</u> <u>God moved</u> upon the face of the waters. The Hebrew word moved: means to brood. What is the purpose of brooding? A chicken broods over her eggs for what purpose? To bring forth life! What is the role of the Holy Spirit? To Quicken or give life.

The minister that said: how can God create darkness if there's no darkness in Him? Has not read the truth of

Isa.45:7. It says "…I form the light, and create darkness: I make peace, and create evil: I the Lord do all these things.

Please read Genesis chapter 2 starting with verse 4-8, God gave us a full history of the heavens and the earth when they were created. The Father never said anything about a gap! If God didn't reveal it, why are some trying to teach it as truth?

Deut.29:29 Says, "…The secret things belong unto the Lord our God: but those things which are revealed belong to us and to our children forever, that we may do all the words of this law". Everything God wants us to know is in His word. This is a violation of scripture! They are adding to the word of God. There are many scriptures, but I like the simplicity of Proverbs 30:5&6 Says, "…Every word Of God is pure: He is a shield unto them that put their trust in him. [6] Add thou not unto his words, lest He reprove you, and you be found a liar.

LET'S GO A LITTLE DEEPER: ADAM

Have you ever heard someone say: if it wasn't for Adam we wouldn't be in all this mess, or if Adam hadn't sinned we wouldn't be in this or that situation!

I want to show you what that statement is really saying!!! Indirectly that statement says that Jesus was Gods alternant plan; just in case Adam sin. They make it sound as if Adam hadn't sinned he would have reached some kind of Spiritual utopia or something.

Listen: it was never Gods plan or intent for righteousness to come by way or through Adam. I firmly believe that we won't have an accurate understanding without the correlation of scripture.

I want to suggest to you that in Adam's case sin was inevitable: it was something that couldn't be avoided or escaped.

When you read and understand Rev.13:8 the last part of that verse, says that "…Jesus was the Lamb slain from the foundation of the world". That means His suffering and our redemption was predetermined before Adam was created. Some make it sounds like Adam became carnal or unspiritual after he sinned, but scripture shows us that he was carnal or unspiritual before he sinned. So there was no way he could keep Gods laws or commandments. Why? Because they are Spiritual!

1st.cor.15:45-49 in these verses the Holy Spirit removes all the drama and gets right to the facts. We use the term: the fall of man, but you won't find that term in scripture, here is what you will find.

Verse 45: "and so it is written, the first man Adam was made a living soul; the last Adam was made a Quickening Spirit".

Verse 46: "Howbeit that was not first which is Spiritual, but that which is natural; and afterward that which is spiritual".

Verse 47: "The first man is of the earth, earthy: The second man is the Lord from heaven".

Verse 48: "as is the earthy, such are they also that are earthy and as is the heavenly such are they also that are heavenly".

How are they that are earthy? Job 4:19 "…They dwell in houses of clay, whose foundation is the dust. Psa.89:48 "what man is he that lives and shall not see death"? He is subject to death, destined to die, worldly minded—devoted to the matters, concerns, interests, or pleasures of this world. Verse 49: "and as we have borne the image of the earthy we shall also bear the image of the heavenly". In contrast, how are they that are heavenly? According to Eph.1:5: "they are spiritually adopted". Verse 13: "We were sealed with the Holy Spirit of promise". According to Gal.4:6 "…Because we are sons, God has sent forth the Spirit of his Son into our hearts crying Abba Father". Giving us the ability to become Spiritual minded through His word: gaining the peace and rest of God.

Now with that in mind, let's look at this natural or carnal man versus the law or the commandments. Genesis 2:16, we see this carnal man commanded by God: saying, of every tree of the garden thou may freely eat. But of the tree of the knowledge of good and evil thou shall not eat of it. For in the day that thou eat there of thou shall surely die.

In Genesis 3:7 we see this command was disobeyed, with the results being death. This is what Paul was referring to in Romans 5:12&14: "…By this one act of disobedience sin entered into the world and death by sin, and so death passed upon all man, for (or because) of that all have sinned. Verse 14: "Never the less death reigned from Adam to Moses, even over them that had not sinned after the similitude of Adam's transgression, who was a figure of Him that was to come.

How was he a figure of him that was to come? Here's the answer: Through Adam's one act of disobedience sin and death entered into the world. Through Jesus one act of obedience the righteousness of God came into the world. Why did death reign from Adam to Moses?

Because Moses was the law giver; the B part of verse 13 says that sin is not imputed where there's no law. Like Paul said in Romans 7:9 I was alive without the law once: but when the commandments came, sin revived, and I dead. Verse 14 reveals exactly what I'm saying! Paul said the law is Spiritual: but I am Carnal, sold under sin. Father: I thank you for sending your Son Jesus to pay the penalty for sin and giving us the abundant Life.

LET'S GO A LITTLE DEEPER:
A LIFE CHANGING INSIGHT

I was reading the book of Isaiah chapter 30 one day and the word 'Egypt' just stood out. So I began to do a word study on it, and I received a lot of insight from what was revealed! The information had such an impact on me I put it into print, and hopefully others will benefit from this inspired word. Now would be a good time for you to stop and pray. Ask God the Holy Spirit to open your eyes to these truths. I am praying they will have a life changing effect on you also.

There are four different views of the word "Egypt" but for the sake of this teaching I will only deal with two of them. The Objective and the Abstract: The word Egypt means: something hemming in or to surround or enclose.

I was born and raised in the small town of Winnfield La., so I'm going to use an example from my youth to give some clarity to this scenario. My mother would tell us to go and catch some chickens and put them in the coop for purification. That was not an easy job at all, but after a few bruises we got smart. We would throw feed into the corner of the yard, and as they all began to eat, we would surround them. This made our objective: to capture them much easier.

We're kind of like the Chickens, just roaming through life with no purpose, easily devoured. God our Father's objective is to capture us with His unconditional love, His kindness, forgiveness, His grace, mercy and truth.

Troubling as it may be to realize, our adversary the devil also has an objective. He wants to entangle us with fleshly pleasures. Especially sensual pleasures: Once you are introduced to sensual pleasures of any kind it leaves a mark that has the potential to be very ugly. It can be a gateway for debauchery, which means: Excessive indulgence in sensual pleasures.

Look at the way our young ladies dress today; it's all about sensuality. Ladies please hear this: Satan is using a lot of fashion designers to undress our beautiful young and innocent girls, and shame on the parents that allow their daughters to dress like that.

What's even more disturbing: I'll show you from the word of God how Satan uses the same position: which is a high place, the same method, which are words and they both target the simple. It's even recorded in the book of Isaiah. Satan says "I will be like the Most High". Read Isaiah chapter 14 starting at verse 12 through 17, and see what God our Father has to say about that!

Let's look at the word 'Egypt' from an Objective view, it means: a Mound of besiegers. The word "mound" means an elevation or a high place. The word "besiegers" means to surround with armed forces in order to capture. Some of you might agree that words are the most powerful forces in the world it just depends on how they are used. God our Father wants to surround us with His word which is the absolute truth: to change our thinking. He wants us to renew our minds with His word, which will deliver us from the blindness we suffered while in unbelief.

I'm going to give you an insight of 2nd Cor.4:3-6 "If our Gospel be hid, it is hid to them that are lost: In whom the god of this world his blinded the minds of them that believe not". Did you get that? Satan has blinded the minds of them that believe not.

Read this very carefully! We were all an unbeliever at one time. We were all blinded, and in our state of blindness we suffered many forms of abuse. This abuse caused us to be rude and unkind! We suffered many forms of betrayal: which lead to a life of falsehood and arrogance and on and on. We suffered many ill things in our state of blindness; and in the darkness of his (Satan) hate, we were destined for destruction. But that Scripture continues, saying, "… Lest the light of this glorious Gospel of Christ, who is the image of God: should shine unto them". Verse 6 is the kicker, "For God, who commanded the light to shine out of darkness, has shined in our hearts to give the light of the knowledge of the glory of God in the face of Jesus Christ". So in the light of God's love, we are now destined for eternity with Him.

The next two topics: The Rampart of love and the Rampart of hate. I'm going to show you how Satan tries to imitate God our Father. However, Satan's methods can only bring forth corruption. All you need is to know and live the truth and you can be an over comer!! But Humans don't inherently know the truth, and unless someone reveals the truth to us: we will go into destruction. God our Father wants us to know and receive His love.

LET'S GO A LITTLE DEEPER:
A RAMPART OF LOVE

Let's start with the definition of Rampart: It means, an embankment, built for defense, or anything that serves as a defense, protection, or an elevation. Now let's go to the word of God and since we're focusing on the Rampart of Love; let's look at Gods position, method, and phraseology and His love for the simple. We can safely say that wisdom typifies Jesus…

Scripture says in 1st. Cor. 1:30 Jesus is made unto us Wisdom, Sanctification, and Redemption. Let's begin in the book of Proverbs 9:1-6 which states that: "Wisdom has built her house. She has hewn out her seven pillars. She has killed her beast and furnished her table. She has sent forth her maiden. She cries upon the highest places of the city. Who so is simple, let him turn in hither; as for him that want understanding, she says to him, come, eat of my bread, and drink of the wine which I have mingled. Forsake the foolish and live; and go in the way of understanding". Look at verse 3 again, it says "she cries upon the highest places, or mound, or an elevation of the city—to give wise and sound instructions to the simple. Wisdom is telling us to eat of the bread, and drink of the wine which she has mingled.

This typifies Jesus because He is the bread of life. It also typifies the Holy Spirit: because He is the only one who can satisfy our thirst. Most importantly of all, Wisdom tells the simple how to acquire wisdom and understanding. Listen to how the Amplified Bible reads in Proverbs 9:10, "The reverent and worshipful fear of the Lord is the beginning, the chief, and choice part of wisdom, and the knowledge of the Holy one is insight and understanding".

The fear of the Lord is the beginning of wisdom, but it is the knowledge of God that gives you insight and understanding. 2nd Peter 1:13, "According as his divine power hath given unto us all things that pertain unto life and godliness, through the knowledge of Him that called us to glory and virtue". (Please continue to read verses 4-11) it will benefit you!

Take note to the Places from where wisdom speaks: the highest places of the city. Her method: Her words. Her phraseology: the way it's said. And who she's addressing: the simple.

The purpose of wisdom is to build a wall of protection around the simple with the truth; to elevate them to a higher place, and God has given us His Spirit to take us to that higher place. Eph. 2:6 says it like this, "God has raised us up together, and made us sit together in heavenly places in Christ Jesus…" To deliver the simple from the corruption that is in the world through lust; and to give them the abundant life and an expected or hopeful end.

LET'S GO A LITTLE DEEPER:
A RAMPART OF HATE

In contrast to wisdom, the foolish woman typifies the world or the spirit of wickedness. According to Proverbs 9:13-17 "She is clamorous or loud: She is simple and knows nothing". Verse 14: she sits at the door of her house on a seat in the high places of the city, to calls passengers who go right on their ways "Whoso is simple, let him turn in hither: and as for him that want understanding she says to him, "stolen waters are sweet and bread eaten in secret is pleasant". I mean she gives the simple nothing but a hard way to go! But that's the world, it's big, it's loud and it offers many opportunities that lead to destruction and false hope. You must understand that everything Satan dose: it is to distract you from receiving the truth. God our Father gives the simple His love and promise of eternal life.

It is very important to note: that she's talking to the simple, and as they are unaware of Satan's plans, they nonchalantly, unknowingly go into destruction.

To make matter even worse, when they look to the Church, they hear of Pastors having sex with their secretaries; Pastors coming out of the closet, having sex with other men; children being sexually abused; a higher divorce rate in the church than that of the world! The simple don't know that wide is the gate; and broad is the way that leads to destruction. So they continue down broad way where everyone seems to be having such a good time. Verse 18: says they don't know that the <u>dead</u> are there; and her guests are in the depths of hell.

Take a look at verse 8 again: and you will see that God placed wisdom in the highest places of the city. Wisdom cries to the simple, forsake the foolish in live and go in the way of understanding. Children of God the Church is suppose to be a bright light: to draw them that go on their ways. But her light has become so dim the simple don't even notice it.

The foolish woman, which typifies the world, has the attention of the simple. Not because she has a bright light, or even the goods: but because she is loud. She doesn't need to be in the highest places to get their attention. She knows that she can keep them entertained by magnifying all the bad things that's happening in the church, and keep them distracted with noise.

Look at the kid today: their music is so loud it will have your car vibrating 10 feet away. It's the noise that keeps them distracted and the dimming light of the Church: keeps them confused. The simple in their confusion will try to fill that void with everything accept the Truth: and Jesus is the Way, the <u>Truth</u> and the life and he is the only one who can feel that void. This is why it is so important to have a personal and vibrant relationship with God the Holy Spirit through our Lord Jesus Christ, to help them see the Truth. Because Satan's sole purpose is to build an embankment of misery and despair, even as a believer.

I do believe Christian's need to hear this again and again. Why? Because I have talk to many Christians that don't seem to understand or have a clue to what Satan is really after, and we will deal with that later.

LET'S GO A LITTLE DEEPER: EXPOSING THE ILL'S OF THE SOUL

The truth is the only thing that exposes all the ills of the soul.

Paul said in Roman 7:7, "…I had not known sin, but by the law: I had not known lust, until the law said thou shall not covet".

It was Romans 7:8 that revealed the power of sin: "But sin taking opportunity by the Commandments, wrought in me all manner of concupiscence". Concupiscence: a very interesting word, this word stresses the lust, Carvings, Longings or Desires for what is usually forbidden. It is an irrational longing for pleasure, unbridled lust. Now that opens up a whole spectrum of things that I will not expound on. But the tenth commandment exposes all of what only God can see.

Without the commandments sin was not recognized: Scripture tell us in Romans 5:13, "…Until the Law sin was in the world, but sin is not Imputed when there's no Law. The purpose of the Law or commandments: were to show man-kind his boundaries; because his ways were offensive to God! The commandments fulfilled its purpose which was to show mankind the power of sin.

Man judges the outward appearance: we look at people and we think or say they are this or that. But God judges the heart; and this is what God said in Jer.17:9-10: "The heart is deceitful above all things. (We can fool the people) and desperately wicked: (it can devise all kind of wicked plans or Schemes) who can know the heart"? Verse 10: "I the Lord search the heart, and try the reins even to give every man according to his ways and according to the fruit of his doing". But our God is full of compassion: He said in Ezekiel 36:26-27: "A new heart also will I give you, and a new spirit will I put within you: and I will take away the stony heart out of your flesh, and give you a heart of flesh". Verse 27: "…and I will put my Spirit within you, and cause you to walk in my statues, and you shall keep my judgments, and do them". The only thing that will take us to that place is His word which is the absolute Truth. We play a big rolled in this process by studying to show ourselves approved unto God. His word will give you the victory over these three forces: 1. The lust of the flesh: that is a craving for sensual gratification. 2. The lust of the eyes: Greedy longings of the mind. 3. The pride of life: The assurance in one's own resources or in the stability of earthly things. That is the scope of his arsenal, but it is very vast, especially to the carnal minds.

LET'S GO A LITTLE DEEPER:

FOREORDAINED

Scripture has pointed out that Jesus was the lamb slain before or from the foundation of the world. 1st Peter 1:18-20

Verse 18: says that, "…We were not redeemed with corruptible things, as silver and gold, from your vain conversation received by tradition from your fathers; But with the precious blood of Jesus Christ, as of a lamb without blemish and without spot.

Verse 20: Who verily was foreordained before the foundation of the world, but was manifest in these last times for you.

Let's look at the word "foreordained": it means to designate before hand to a position or functions. In the councils of the triune God, the Lord Jesus was the Lamb marked out for sacrifice. The word 'foundation' is the translation of a word meaning, literally to throw down, and was used of the laying of the foundation of a house. It speaks of the act of the transcendent God throwing out into space or the universe by speaking the word. The word "world" in the text is ("kosmos"), which speaks of the creator before the universe was created: the Lord Jesus had been foreordained to be the savior of lost sinners. The saints has been foreordained to become recipients of the salvation He would procure or cause to be in effect for lost sinners at the cross, Eph.1:4.

Let's look at one more word, Decree: one of the eternal purposes of God, by which events are foreordained. God didn't just look down from heaven and said, oh they don't believe, hell will freeze over before they enter into my rest! No, He made a decree from the foundation of the world, and it's waiting for all who would believe, and if we believe according to scripture His rest is inevitable. When I got saved I didn't know anything about the rest, peace, and the joy of the Lord. I wasn't seeking rest, but I met the requirements for his rest, and it is so real!

Jesus made a decree that shall stand forever in John 10:9, I am the door: by me if any Man Enter in, he shall be saved, and shall go in and out, and find pasture. In the Greek the word Sozo means to deliver or protect, heal preserve to make whole: which is the complete rest of God.

LET'S GO A LITTLE DEEPER: REALLY?

It amazes me how a Christian will take another Christian to law for whatever reason, and if they win the case they praise God for the victory.

But God is not pleased with that kind of action. The Spirit of God said through Paul in 1stCor. 6:1-4&7, "… Dare any of you that have a matter against another, go to law before the unjust, and not before the saints.

1. Do you not know that the saints will judge the world? And if the world will be judged by you are you unworthy to judge the smallest matter?

2. Do you not know that we shall judge angels? How much more things that pertain to this life?

3. If then you have judgments concerning things pertaining to this life, do you appoint those who are least esteemed in the church to judge? A very interesting question: "Do you appoint those who are least esteemed in the church".

4. Then he said, "I say this to your shame". I believe they that are least esteemed in the church will show mercy and fairness in a matter. But Paul continues by saying: "…is it so, that there is not a wise man among you, not even one, who will be able to judge between his brethren?

5. But brother goes to law against brother, and that before the unbelievers.

6. Now therefore, it is already an utter failure for you that you go to law against one another. Why do you not rather accept wrong? Why do you not rather let yourself be cheated? Nay you yourselves do wrong and cheat, and you do those things to your brethren. So accept the wrong if that be the case and remember: our Heavenly Father sees all and knows all, so you can walk away with full confidence knowing that God have your back!!

LET'S GO A LITTLE DEEPER: THE ABSTRACT METHOD OF THE ENEMY

In this method I'm about to share with you, literally no one is exempt. The truth is all we have and need to combat this method, so let's start with some definitions. The word "Abstract" means: to conceive or consider apart from matter. The word "Conceive" means: to form or develop mentally; plan, devise: to have or form a mental image or ideal of. Now it gets more intense: This last definition for the word 'Abstract' is the one that lines up with what I want to share: to become pregnant with. This abstract method derives as a thought or an ideal and it is for that very reason the enemy uses this method so effectively, and again the truth is our weapon of warfare.

Now we must understand that we are in direct conflict with unseen entities: something with real and distinct existence. This is why we are admonished to be strong in the Lord and in the power of His might.

How do you do that? Eph.6:11, States that you do it by putting on the whole armor of God, and it starts by having your loins girt about with the <u>Truth</u>. He could have said: having your loins girt about with Faith or righteousness. But it is the <u>Truth</u> that activates the breastplate of righteousness, your feet shod with the preparation of the Gospel of peace, the Shield of Faith, the Helmet of Salvation; are all activated by the sword of the Spirit, which is the word of God, which is the absolute truth: that you may be able to stand against the wiles, schemes and plots of the devil.

Here's why this is so important: Eph.6:12 says, "… we wrestle not against flesh and blood, but we do wrestle against principalities, powers, rulers of the darkness of this world, spiritual wickedness in high places.

What are "Principalities"? They are rulers in general particularly angels and demons, but including earthly magistrates or rulers.

What are "magistrates"? Government officers empowered to administer and enforce the law. Spiritual wickedness: denotes the active exercise of a vicious disposition. Powers: denotes the power of rule or government, the power of one whose will and commands must be obeyed by others. This is why we need the Truth to stand against these wiles and schemes of the enemy. As you can see He comes in many different forms. Therefore it is vital that we know the truth. Just being exposed to the truth is not going to help you stand in the evil day, and we all have them! Jesus said you shall know the truth and the truth will make you free.

Here's my point: you will not be able to use your spiritual authority unless you know the truth, and you won't know the truth just by reading.—We are instructed to study to show ourselves approved unto God!

I will repeat: this method doesn't have anything to do with the physical realm: it derives as a thought or an ideal. This is how James 1:14-15 explains it, and it reveals what the individual has been dwelling on. It says, [14]"…Every man is temped, when he is drawn away of his own lust and enticed". His own lust, something he's been dwelling on. [15] "Then when lust has conceived, it brings forth sin: and sin when it is finished, bring forth death". In order to really see this you must understand that the Spirit of God is identifying lust as a separate entity from the body, and it reveals how lust or a strong desires, uses the body to bring forth corruption.

Listen closely to this metaphor: most of us understand the process of how a woman conceives a child, sperm and egg connects and conception takes place. Then after a nine month period, this woman is going to bring forth a human, be it boy or girl. In the same way, when lust is conceived it bring forth sin, and sin: if allowed to run it full course: brings forth death!

We know thoughts conceived has built entire cities, sent man to the moon, Advanced technology, among many wonderful things. But thoughts conceived has also caused so must pain and sorrow. That's what Paul is referring to: that which brings forth death. Notice how he began that statement! "Every man is tempted when he is drawn away of his own lust and enticed". Mark 7:21-22 gives us a full description of what is in us, [21]"For from within, out of the heart of man proceed: evil thoughts, adulteries, fornications, murders. [22] "…Thefts, covetousness, an evil eye, blasphemy, pride, foolishness: all these evil things come from within, and defile the man. All of these ills are in the heart or soul of man, and they govern his thoughts. The remedy is in obeying the truth, and it's noticeable. Listen closely to 1st Peter 1:22 "Seeing you have purified your souls in obeying the truth through the Spirit unto unfeigned love of the brethren. See that you love one another with a pure heart fervently". Did you get that? I can see that you have purified your souls in obeying the truth. Now that you are capable, love one another with a pure heart. What I want you to see is your soul must to be purified.

The soul is the principle of life! Genesis 2:7 says, God formed man from the dust of the ground and breathed into his nostrils the breath of life and man became a living soul. The soul: consisting of the faculties of thoughts, emotions, and actions, and regarded as a separate entity distinct from the body. Now with that in mind, let me say it this way. Seeing you have purified your thoughts, emotions, and actions in obeying the truth through the Spirit; see those faculties have to be purified or washed with the truth. Otherwise those thoughts, emotions, and actions will manifest in the physical realm through this method.

I believe this is the primary reason we are admonished to take control of our thoughts. 1st Peter 1:13 "…Therefore gird up the loin of your mind, be sober, and rest your hope fully upon the grace that is to be brought to you at the revelation of Jesus Christ. In Philippians 4:8 we are told what to think on, "whatsoever things that are true, honest, just, pure, lovely and of a good report. If there be any virtue or praise, think on these things". 2nd Corinthians 10:5 Casting down imaginations, and every high thing that exalts itself against the knowledge of God, and bring into captivity every though to the obedience of Christ; and we have the God given power to do that.

Here are some things to consider: The mind that has not been renewed typifies lust ovaries: it produces or creates thoughts and images. The imagination typifies lust ovulating: it discharges all of those emotions and feelings of past experiences and present desires. The enticement typifies the sperm. We know a woman doesn't conceive every time she receives the male sperm. Conception can only take place when the sperm and egg connects. Likewise, you don't respond to every enticement. But, when enticement connects with thoughts or Emotions—which typifies the egg—conception takes place and you will bring forth Corruption.

Let's look at a few scriptures dealing with conceiving. Psalm 7:14 "Behold, he travails with iniquity, and has conceived mischief, and brought forth falsehood". The amplified bible is very blunt, it says "…the wicked man conceives iniquity and is pregnant with mischief and give birth to lies" Job 15:35 says, "They conceived mischief and bring forth iniquity, and their inmost soul hatches deceit". Children of God please understand this, When conception takes place just resisting is not enough. I will repeat: we are instructed to first submit, and then resist.

LET'S GO A LITTLE DEEPER: WHY SUBMIT?

Submitting is the only way out. The word "submit" means to subordinate: which means to come under or subject unto the higher power. Romans 13:1, "…Let every soul be subject unto the higher powers. For there is no power but of God: the powers that be are ordained of God. The word "submit" was originally a Greek military term meaning to arrange in a military fashion, under the command of a leader. But, in a non-military use, it means a voluntary attitude of giving in, cooperating, assuming responsibility, and carrying a burden.

Submitting will be the harder of the two! Why? Because the individual now has this entity existing inside his soul! It's going to manifest in the physical realm, and it's going to bring pleasure to your flesh in some form. If you want this thing to be properly aborted, you must take on the attitude of giving in and cooperate with the word of God. Assume responsibility, and confess that this conception was of your own doing. Then carry the burden for allowing it to cause you to sin. After you've done this, you can resist with confidence.

WHY RESIST?

You resist because Satan doesn't want you to abort his offspring; corruption. He's going to do everything in his power to encourage you to bring forth that little ugly thing. If lust is allowed to run its full term or completion, then death is the result! Death of a marriage, death of a ministry and all the people that are affected, death of trust, death of your name! Please understand this: you don't have to give birth to that little ugly thing called corruption! You can come under the protective hand of God and of your own will resist the devil and he will flee James 4:7. But you can't stop there, because lust is still carrying that little ugly thing. You must now confess your sins to God and He will cleanse you, and stop lust from giving birth to corruption. (1st John 1:9): And that scripture is not to be abused.

LET'S GO A LITTLE DEEPER: INORDINATE AFFECTION

Earlier I was talking about bringing forth so please give this topic your undivided attention! I want to show you the effects caused by abuse. Let's look at the words "Inordinate Affection". These words primarily denote whatever one experiences in anyway which affects him hence, an affection of the mind which stimulates a passionate desire or capricious delight. The disease of passion—always used in a bad sense—primarily denotes whatever one suffers or experiences.

I do understand that mental illness is real. But, a lot of what we are seeing is not mental illness, its "Inordinate Affection" brought on by physical or mental abuse. After many studies and observations they found that most serial killers where abused as a child. Earlier in the book we defined the word "conceived", and one of the definitions means to develop mentally. When you abuse a child you are stimulating a passionate desire that will develop into a disease of passion. We are seeing these mass killings and saying how can someone be so heartless to do something like that?

This is "Inordinate Affection", and they were not born that way, they developed into that through a channel call abuse. We are warned in Eph.6:4 "…provoke not your children to wrath; but bring them up in the nurture and admonition of the Lord". Col.3:21 reveal's the danger of violating this scripture. "Father Provoke not your children to anger, lest they become <u>"Discouraged"</u>.

Let's look at some more definitions, which will give us a better understanding. The word discouraged in the Greek means: Athumeo which means: to be "<u>Disheartened</u> or <u>Dispirited</u>". "Disheartened" means: to lose hope, depress, discouraged. The B part of Eph.6:4 say's, "but bring them up in the fear and admonition of the Lord.

Scripture is very clear on this issue.

Prov.22:6 Says, Train up a child in the way he should go, and when he is old, he will not depart from it. I know many of you know this scripture by memory, but have you ever meditated on that scripture? I must admit, the definition took me for a Spin. The word "train" means to narrow. I'm going to give this scripture first, and then my point of view. Matt.7:13-14 "Enter by the narrow gate; for wide is the gate and broad is the way that leads to destruction, and there are many who go in by it. Because narrow is the gate and difficult is the way which leads to life, and there are few who find it.

When you are training a child, you are narrowing his options. While in training he's learning this is wrong and will never be accepted or this is right and will always be approved. What are you doing? You are making a straight path to life, and when he or she is old they won't depart from it. There's a catch to it: it must be done by example. You can't say do as I say and not as I do: that will not go over too well. Children don't need to be confused while developing, like a lot of us were!

LET'S GO A LITTLE DEEPER: PROVERBS 6:16 THESE SIX THINGS GOD HATES AND SEVEN IS AN ABOMINATION

The first of these is a proud look: Psa.101:5 "Him that has a high look and a proud heart will I not suffer". Psa.138:6 "Though the Lord is high, yet hath he respect unto the lowly but the proud He knows afar off". Prov.16:5 "Every one that is proud is an abomination to the Lord: though hand, join in hand, he shall not go unpunished.

There are many examples in the word of God: Let's take a look at King Uzziah in 2nd Chronicles 26:15-21. Please read the whole story starting in verse one.

Uzziah became King at the age of sixteen and He reigned fifty two years, and he did what was right in the sight of God. He had 2,000 mighty man of valor and under their hands, was an army of 307,500 that help the king against the enemy. The last part of verse 15: say, "…his fame spread far abroad; for he was marvelously helped, till he was strong. [16] "But when he was strong, his heart was lifted up to his destruction: for He transgressed against the Lord his God, and went into the temple of the Lord to burn incense upon the Alter of incense". [17:] "Azariah the Priest took eighty Priests of the Lord, man of courage.

[18:] They opposed King Uzziah, "saying it is not for you, Uzziah to burn incense to the Lord. The sons of Aaron are consecrated to burn incense; and told him to get out of the sanctuary because you have trespassed; neither shall it be for their honor from the Lord God". [19:] "Uzziah became very angry and had a Censer in his hand to burn incense: While he was angry with the Priest the leprosy even rose up in his forehead". Uzziah was a leper until the day of his death. I must say this again: Porverbs.16:5 every one that is proud is an abomination to the Lord, though hand join in hand, he shall not go unpunished.

LET'S GO A LITTLE DEEPER:
A LYING TONGUE, AND HANDS
THAT SHED INNOCENT BLOOD

I'm going to put these next two points together because this next story reveals the detriment of lying.

Psa.63:11, "...the king shall rejoice in God; every one that swears by him shall glory: but the mouth of them that speak lies shall be stopped". Proverbs 19:5: "A false witness shall not be unpunished, and he that speaks lies shall not escape".

Rev.21:8 Says, "...The fearful, and unbelieving, and the abominable, and murderers, and whoremongers, and sorcerers, and idolaters, and <u>all</u> <u>liars</u> shall have their part in the lake which burns with fire and brimstone which is the second death".

A lying spirit has infiltrated the oval office, but the word of God says the mouth of them that speak lies shall be stopped.

There is a very interesting story in 1ˢᵗ.Kings 21 through chapter 22. (Please read the whole story).

Naboth the Jezreelite had a vineyard which was in Jezreel, next to the Palace of Ahab King of Samaria. Ahab asked Naboth to give him his vineyard, because it was near his home: and he wanted to grow vegetables in it. He offered to give him a better one or give him the wroth in money.

V.3 "…Naboth said to Ahab the Lord for bid it me, that I should give the inheritance of my father unto you.

Ahab was very displeased with his answer. V.5 Jezebel his wife came to him, and said, "…why is thy spirit so sad, and thou eat no bread"? Ahab said: "because Naboth won't give me the vineyard".

V.7 Jezebel said to him, do you not govern Israel? Arise and eat bread and let your heart be happy. I will give you the vineyard of Naboth the Jezreelite. She then fabricated a lie against Naboth by writing letters in Ahab's name and sealed them with his seal and sent them to the elders and nobles who dwelt with Naboth in his city. In the letters she said, proclaim a fast and set two base fellows before him, and let them, be a witness against him. Saying he cursed and did blasphemed God and the king. Then he was carried out of the city and stoned to death. This lie caused a man's death. But God is faithful to fulfill his word. V.16 When Ahab heard that Naboth was dead: Ahab rose up to go to the vineyard of Naboth the Jezreelite, to take possession of it.

V.17 "The word of the Lord came to Elijah the Tish'bite, saying, v.18 "Arise, go down to meet Ahab King of Israel, which is in Samaria: behold, he is in the vineyard of Naboth where he is gone to possess it". [19:] say to him, "…thus says the Lord: Have you killed and also taken possession? Thou shall speak unto him, saying, "Thus says the Lord, in the place where dogs lick the blood of Naboth shall lick your blood, even yours". [20] Ahab replied: "have you found me oh my enemy"? Elijah answered I have found you, because you have sold yourself to do evil in the sight of the Lord. See says the Lord I will bring evil on you and utterly sweep away and cut off from Ahab every male bond and free.

1st Kings 22:1 "…Now Syria and Israel continued without war for three years. In the third year Jehoshaphat King of Judah went down to meet Ahab King of Israel. Ahab said to him: do you know that Ramoth in Gilead is ours. And we keep silence and do not take it from the King of Syria?

Then he asked him will you go with me to Ramoth Gilead to battle? Jehoshaphat said I am as you are my people as your people, my horses as your horses. But inquire first I pray you for the word of the Lord <u>Today.</u> Ahab gathered together 400 Prophets all of whom agreed with him. [V.5] "Jehoshaphat said is there another Prophet of the Lord here whom we may ask"? [V.8] "Ahab said yes there's one more man, Micaiah son of Imlah, by whom we may inquire of the Lord, but I hate him; Because he never prophesy good concerning me, but evil".

[V.13:] The messenger who went to call micaiah said to him. "…Behold now, the Prophets unanimously declare good to the King. Let your answer, I pray you be like theirs, and say what is good. But Micaiah said I will speak what the Lord says to me. [V.15] He took him to the King and the King asked him, "…shall we go against Ramoth Gilead to battle or hold back"? Micaiah said go and proper for the Lord will deliver it into your hand.

V.16 Then Ahab said "…how many times, must I charge you to tell me nothing but the truth in the name of the Lord". Now please get this: King Ahab asked for the truth, but listen to his response to the truth.

V.17 Micaiah gives him the truth: "…saying I saw all Israel scattered upon the hills as sheep that had no Shepherd, and the Lord said, these have no master. Let them return every man to his house in peace.

V.18 Ahab said to Jehoshaphat, "…did I not tell you that he would prophesy no good concerning me, but evil"?

V.19 Micaiah said "…hear the word of the Lord. (Now you will get a glimpse of how the Heavenly realm operates). I saw the Lord sitting on His throne, and all the host of heaven standing by him on his right hand and on the left. Then the Lord asked a question. Who will I send to persuade Ahab to go up and fall at Ramoth-gilead? One said on this manner, and one said on that manner. V.21 and there came forth a spirit, and stood before the Lord, and said, "I will persuade him". V.22 "…And the Lord said unto him, wherewith? And he said, I will go forth, and I will be a <u>Lying Spirit</u> in the mouth of all his prophets. And he said thou shall persuade him, and prevail also: go forth, and do so. Please read the rest of that chapter so you can see Ahab's fall. But this is what I want you to see: His wife Jezebel fabricated lies which cause a man's life, and God used a lying spirit to take her husband Ahab's life. Proverbs 6:16 the first three things God hates is 1. A proud look! 2. A lying tongue! 3. Hands that shed innocent blood! He did all three of them.

A heart that devise wicked imaginations. Roman 1:21 "When they knew God, they glorified him not as God, neither were thankful; but became vain in their imagination, and their foolish heart was darkened".

Feet that is swift in running to mischief. Proverbs 4:16 "For they sleep not, except they have done mischief: and their sleep is taken away, unless they cause someone to fall".

A false witness that speak lies. Proverbs 12:17 "He that speaks the truth shows forth righteousness: but a false witness deceit". Proverbs 19:9. "A false witness shall not be unpunished, and he that speaks lies shall perish".

This 7th one: 'Sowing Discord' among brethren is an abomination to God. What is an abomination? Something disgusting.

The Hebrew word <u>Toebah</u> defines something or someone as essentially unique in the sense of being dangerous, sinister, and repulsive to another individual. When used with reference to God, this word describes people, things, acts, relationships, and characteristics that are detestable to him because they are contrary to His nature; such things that relates to death and idolatry. Here is a warning from Job 4:8 "Even as I have seen, they that plow iniquity, and sow wickedness, reap the same". Proverbs 6:14 "<u>Frowardness</u> is in his heart, he devise mischief continually; he sows discord".

LET'S GO A LITTLE DEEPER: WHAT IS SATAN REALLY AFTER? FAITH & LOVE!

If you are thinking that Satan's only objective is to get you to sin: then you are sadly mistaken. I even hear people say, he wants to steal your testimony. That might be true, but he has his sight on something much bigger. A large percentage of the Body of Christ doesn't have a clue to what he is after!

There are two major fruit Satan wants to pillage—Faith and Love, and here are the primary reasons. Satan knows that the armor of faith is the only thing that can quench all his fiery darts. Eph.6:16 "above all, taking the shield of Faith, wherewith you shall be able to quench all the fiery darts of the wicked". He also knows that without Faith it is impossible to please God. Hebrews 11:6 "Without Faith it is impossible to please Him: He that comes to God must believe that He is and that He is a <u>Rewarder</u> of them that diligently seek Him".

Secondly, he wants to keep us from walking in genuine love. Why? Because Faith works by Love! The last part of Gal.5:6 Paul says "that in Christ the only thing that is of value or worth, is Faith which works by love".

I'm going to give you another metaphor: let me make this clear, this is a metaphor, not a new teaching on faith.

I must tell you that I'm an observer: I went to a word of faith church one Sunday and observed something that put me on a search for answers. This is what I observed: This church had a guest speaker that day and before he finished speaking he stated: if there's anyone in here that's being tormented by a spirit of fear come forward and I will pray for you, and over half the church came up for prayer.

I thank God for that brother being sensitive to the spirit, and the people that were honest enough to respond. But, according to the word of God something was desperately wrong with that picture. 2nd Timothy 1:7 says, "God has not given us a spirit of fear, but of power, love and of a sound mind". Jesus addressed the issue concerning fear in Matt.6:30, & 8:26, and 16:18. In each case he ended his statement with the phrase, "Oh ye of little Faith". Two places in particular, "why are you fearful, oh ye of little faith"? "Why did you doubt, oh ye of little of faith"? That tells me that fear and doubting are a result of little or a lack of faith!

The word 'little faith' in those two verses means a lack of confidence in Christ. Now, we need to consider something here. Why? Because this took place in a so called "Word of Faith Church"! The Pastor is an excellent teacher: so what's the problem? Maybe it's that, faith is more than something you use to try and get things from God. That's what "faith" seems to be in a lot of those churches. They have their little books of confessions, and their confessions are centered on getting things, which has nothing to do with faith.

Scripture is very clear on how to get things! Matt.6:33 "you seek first the Kingdom of God and His righteousness; and all these things will be added unto you". These things are added as you mature in the things of God! I hope this metaphor will bring some clarity to what faith is and how it comes to us. It was obvious the people hadn't got it: the proof was at the altar. Now I will say this again: this is a metaphor not a new doctrine on faith.

For those of you that might say, I never really understood what a metaphor is, here's the definition. "A figure of speech in which one object: or ideal is compared, or identified with another in order to suggest a similarity between the two".

I was reading Romans 12, which I had read many times, but this time I couldn't get past the third verse. The last part of that verse reads, "according as God has dealt to every man the measure of faith". The way that passage was phrased reminded me of another passage I had read before. As I sat there staring at the verse, the Spirit of God gave me a reference which took me to Gen.2:7 which says, "And the Lord God formed man of the dust of the ground and breathed into his nostrils the breath of life, and he became a living soul". As I began to ponder that, I began saying it over and over to myself, "the breath of life, the measure of faith". That's when I saw the similarity. When you were born physically you received the breath of life, and at that very moment God put two things in operation that will sustain you for a life time: Breathing and the heart-beat, they go hand in hand. Breathing causes the heart to beat which keeps the blood flowing to nourish the trillions of cells in the body, and no one need to teach you how to Breath. As long as you keep the body nourished, breathing won't be a problem, and as you grow physically the capacity for oxygen increases. It's a natural occurrence! It's very important to know that the breath of life was given by God our Father.

In the same manner: when you were born again spiritually, you received the measure of Faith, and at that very moment God put two things in operation that will sustain your spiritual life which will never end. These are Faith and Love. They go hand in hand! Faith is the oxygen and Love is the Heart-beat and as you grow spiritually, the capacity for Faith and Love increases, it's a spiritual occurrence! It is equally important to know that the measure of faith was given by God the Father and only He can cause it to increase as you grow in Him.

Just as the breath of life supports the physical body to do the many things it's able to do, based on the gifts and talents given by God. Romans 12:3 Reveals to us that God gave the measure or the proportion of faith to support the spiritual gifts that are mentioned in verses 6-8 and the many facets of those gifts. I hope through that metaphor you were able to see that faith is more than just a life style or something you use to get things. It is the very oxygen that supports our spiritual life: without it we die.

What I saw was very disturbing!! These churches are filled every Sunday, and faith is the primary subject. So, why is the altar filled with over half the church tormented by a spirit of fear? There may be other reasons but this one is obvious according to scripture. A lack of love!!!

1st John 4:18, "There is no fear in love: but perfect love casts out fear; because fear has torment. He that fears is not made perfect in love". I will repeat Gal.5:6 again, this is the kicker. The last part of that verse says "faith works by love". This is the primary reason faith is not active in the lives of many because they are not walking in genuine love toward the brethren. 1st Peter 1:22 talks about having "unfeigned love for the brethren…" which means: not pretend or hypocritical but genuine, sincere love for one another.

I made a statement earlier about how everything you've ever experienced is lodged in the soul. Think about it, a life time of good and bad experiences. If the soul is not purified by obeying the truth through the spirit you won't be able to love genuinely, you won't allow yourself to be vulnerable. There's always a wall to protect your emotions. I hope you can see that you can't have genuine love without being vulnerable. When genuine love is in operation: there's always a chance of getting hurt or wounded, Jesus was and is our example.

Just as the heart can't function without breathing, faith can't function without love. Habakkuk 2:4, "The just shall 'Live' by Faith". Just as the physical body lives by breathing, your Spiritual body lives by Faith! Faith is your spiritual breath of live. As you grow and mature in the things of God through obeying the truth: the soul is being purified and the unfeigned love of God fills your heart.

If the soul is not being purified through obeying the truth: then genuine love lies dormant, and if genuine love lies dormant faith cannot increase. It's like having asthma you can Breathe: but not fully. But you need your Faith to increase! In order for that to take place genuine love is paramount to cast out all fear.

This genuine love is only acquired through the purifying of the soul in obeying the truth. This will allow the Spirit of God to pour the light of his love into all of those dark places enabling you to breathe fully, spiritually.

A co-worker of mine was rushed to the hospital with a congested heart. When he returned to work I asked him: "what were the symptoms"? His answer was: I couldn't Breathe! That gives this metaphor more validity. Hopefully you can see why Satan, our adversary, wants to pillage these two major fruits. Notice I said pillage, because when a large amount of something is taken you notice it right away. But when real small portions are taken, you won't notice it until it's too late. Your adversary the devil has been pillaging your Love walk. Without love Faith automatically fails.

LET'S GO A LITTLE DEEPER: THE MISCONCEPTION OF FAITH

God didn't put this life giving force called Faith in the hands of man. Why? Because God knew man would exploit it, just as he has done under the guise of a so called movement of God. I'm going to give you a scripture first, and I'm going to share with you the misconception of faith.

If you are a believer I want you to know that this scripture is speaking directly to you. St. John 1:12-13 "But as many as received Him, to them He gave power to become the sons of God, even to them that believe on his name": Now please give close attention to [v13] "Which were born not of blood, nor of the will of the flesh, nor of the will of man, "BUT OF GOD".

It was God who breathed the initial breath of life into man and it was God who dealt to man the measure of faith:

and He's the only one who can increase your Faith. I heard this one pastor say faith is like a muscle, the more you use it the bigger it gets. That statement has no scriptural support!

My question is how do you use Faith? The Greek word 'Pistis' is used more than any word for faith in the Bible. It means: a firm persuasion, a conviction based upon hearing. It's always used of Faith in God, Christ, or Spiritual things.

My point is: you won't find Faith in a book of confessions. Remember this was a so called "Word of Faith" Church and they are steeped in confessions. But yet the altar was filled with over half the church tormented by a spirit of fear. I must add that faith is not positive thinking but, as you grow in God you will have a positive outlook on life!

Let me share something else with you that might shock you. A large percentage of the Body of Christ, are led to believe that faith comes by reading their bible and coming to church to hear the word preached. This is not so, although both are desperately essential. The sad part is they don't realize it until they are being attacked by the enemy. 2nd Tim.3:16 show's us the limitations of the word of God which is extremely vast, but limited. Listen closely as you read! "All scripture is given by inspiration of God, and is profitable for doctrine, for reproof, for correction, for instruction in righteousness". V 17 "That the man of God maybe perfect (or mature) thoroughly furnished unto all good works". But it won't produce faith!

This is why it is so important to have a vibrant and intimate relationship with God the Holy Spirit, because without it the bible is just another book. A very interesting book that will benefit you immensely! But, according to 1st Corinthians 2:14 "…The things of God are spiritually discerned, and again it's limited. Here's why: there are two Greek definitions for word, 'Logos' and "Rhema" The

'Logos' is God's spoken word and His word became flesh and dealt among us: the Logos is (Jesus) and He basically came to teach us kingdom principles, and inspire us to seek the living God not a religion. When you attend church on Sundays to hear the inspired word preached or taught by your Pastor,—now please get this! He received 'Rhema' from God, but when he delivers it to you: I don't care how eloquent or charismatic he or she is, you are getting an inspired word that will benefit you, if you take heed! Please understand this, the 'Logos' will benefit you by way of doctrine or teaching, reproof, rebuke or correction, and for instruction in righteousness that you may be perfect or mature.

I want to draw your attention to the word 'may' because this word is used in some cases to express possibilities or power to do. My point is you may or may not mature in the things of God. I know that to be true in lives of many. They have been exposed to the 'Logos' for years, but never came to a play of maturity! I'm aware that it takes time to come to that place but, that statement still stands true. Here is the purpose of the 'Logos', it's to make you perfect or mature, 'Complete'. This is exactly what Hebrews 4:12 is indicating, "For the 'Logos' or written word of God is Quick and Powerful, and sharper than any two edged sword, piercing even to the dividing asunder of soul and spirit, and the joints and marrow, and is a discerner of the thoughts and intents of the heart". The 'Logos' primary purpose is for us to learn the ways of God to make you aware of the things that will hinder your Spiritual growth, and it is the prerequisite for 'Rhema'. In case you don't know the definition of "prerequisite", here it is: a thing that is required as a prior condition for something else to happen or exist.

Now that you see something is required of you, for something else to happen: Something like studying to show yourself approved unto God! When you study, you don't pass words that you don't understand. No, you make sure you know and understand what the 'Logos' is revealing.

Here are the benefits of storing Scriptures in your heart: This is where ("Rhema") is revealed. God the Holy Spirit is going to take the scriptures that you have stored in your heart and use them as a tool to help you in times of need. To speak "Rhema" to you: to open the eyes of your understanding. It's through those experiences you will encounter through your obedience that your faith will Increases! Romans 10:17 say: Faith comes by hearing and hearing by the word (or "Rhema") of God. It's Preparation: "Rhema" is not a given, it's seeking Him and submitting to His word that you might find the fullness of HIM. Causing a maturity that will cause your faith to be unmovable and always abounding in the things of God, enabling you to encourage others. Here is the good news: God wants to speak to all of us in a clear and personal way, and He's not hiding, he's waiting…!

LET'S GO A LITTLE DEEPER: UNSHAKABLE FAITH OF NOAH AND ABRAHAM

There are many Patriarchs in the Bible, but let's focus on two of them: Noah and Abraham. Let's see what motivated them to stand firm when faced with impossible odds. Hebrews 11:7, "…Noah being warned of God of things not seen as yet, moved with fear, prepared an ark to the saving of his house; by the which he condemned the world, and became heir of the righteousness which is by faith". Genesis 5:32, "…Noah was five hundred years old. Genesis 6:8 Says, "He found grace in the eyes of the Lord in spite of all the wickedness and violence he was surrounded by. Genesis 6:13, "God said unto Noah, the end of all flesh is come before me; for the earth is filled with violence through them; and, behold, I will destroy them with the earth". The Hebrew word for "said" is "Amar" this word refers to the simple act of communicating with the spoken word. It can be used of direct or indirect speech as well. But when used by God it's more than making a statement: It's authoritative, usually with a command or instruction. Genesis6:14-15 "God told him to build an ark, and gave him the dimensions on how to build it. Genesis 6:17, "God told him how He was going to destroy and kill every living thing on the face of the earth". Genesis 6:18-22, "But with thee will I establish my covenant; you and your family shall come into the ark".

God instructed him to take two of every kind of living things, male and female, from cattle to creeping things. He told him to gather food for himself and for the animals. What a task! But we read that Noah did according to all that God commanded him, so did He. A hundred years later when Noah was six hundred, God told him in the 7th chapter of Genesis verse 4, "…in seven days I will cause it to rain for forty days and forty nights". Now think for a moment how Noah must have felt after being criticized daily… You know they mocked him, called him crazy, but he continued to obey God, and now it's about to pay off. Genesis 7:6 Says, "Noah was six hundred when the floods of water was upon the earth. V 11 "In the six hundredth year of Noah's life, the second month, the seventeenth day of the month, the same day were all the fountains of the great deep were broken up, and the windows of heaven were opened". V 13 "…Noah and his family went into the ark. V 16 "…and they went in male and female of all flesh, as God had commanded him: and the Lord shut them in.

Noah was able to stand firm in the face of opposition because God spoke to him personally and he believed God and Obeyed. Because of his obedience God blessed him and his family. You don't get this kind of confidence from just listening to man. He can only give you the inspired word, and it should inspire you to seek the living God. Whom: will cause you to experience Isaiah 40:31. This is from the Amplified Bible: But those who wait for the Lord [who expect, look for, and hope in Him] shall change and renew their strength and power; they shall lift their wings and mount up [close to God] as eagles [mount up to the sun]; they shall run and not be weary, they shall walk and not faint or become tired. That's what Noah experienced from waiting on the Lord!

ABRAHAM

Let's look at the man Abraham, formerly known as Abram. After reading his story, all I can say is wow!! You can see why they called him the father of Faith. It would take too much time to cover everything about Abraham, but read Genesis chapter 15 through chapter 21:1-18 and be amazed again at the awesomeness of God.

I'm going to focus on the revelation the Holy Spirit gave us through Paul in Romans Chapter 4. We then will talk about some of the things that are revealed in Genesis. Romans 4:18 "Who against hope believed in hope, that he might become the Father of many nations, according to that which was spoken, so shall thy seed be. Romans [19] "Being not weak in faith, he considered not his own body now dead, when he was about a hundred years old, neither the deadness of Sarah's womb. [20] "He staggered not at the promises of God through unbelief, but was strong in faith giving glory to GOD; [21] "…and being fully persuaded that what he had promised, He was able also to perform. I'm going to come back to that statement later!

Genesis Chapter 16:16, reveals to us that Abram was 86 years old when he had a son by his hand maid Hager. Thirteen years later, In Genesis 17:1 when he was 99, <u>God</u> talked with him. Verse 5 God changed his name to Abraham. Verse 7 God said to Abraham, "I will establish my covenant between me and thee and thy seed after thee in their generation for an everlasting covenant, to be a God unto thee, and thy seed after thee". Genesis 17:10 God explained to him the terms of the covenant, "…that every male child among you shall be circumcised. [11] "And you shall circumcise thy foreskin; and it will be a token of the covenant between me and you". Then in verses 15-16 God said to Abraham, "as for Sarai thy wife, thou shall not call her name Sarai, but Sarah shall her name be called. [16] And I will bless her, and give thee a son also of her". I always hear people talk about how Sarah laughed, but when you read verse 17 you see Abraham fell upon his face and laughed, and said in his heart, "shall a child be born unto him that is a hundred years old, and Sarah that is ninety years old bear?"

It's been said that Abraham didn't doubt God, and they base it on that statement in Romans 4:20 where it says: "He staggered not at the promises of God through unbelief but was strong in Faith giving glory to God". But in Genesis 17:17 He seem to have questions, which can sound doubtful. What about that statement in verse 18 "Oh that Ishmael might live before thee!"? It might seem like that statement had little or no significance. But it was totally legitimate, because in their culture the inheritance always went to the first born. But God said "no, thy wife Sarah shall bear thee a son".

Personally I believe he doubted at first! (Notice I said personally) because it's my opinion, meaning you can receive it or not. When you know someone and establish a relationship, everything changes; your Heart just knows, and Abraham came to know that He is a God that cannot lie. This is the promise I believe the Holy Spirit is referring to in Romans 4:20-21 where it says, "Abraham staggered not at the promises of God through unbelief, but was strong in faith giving glory to God, and being fully persuaded". Which would or should indicate he was not fully persuaded at first. But understanding who God is, he knew what God had promised He was also able to perform!

Abraham believed God! How do I know that? In Genesis 17:23 it says "Abraham took every male among the men in his house hold and circumcised them, and Abraham was ninety nine years old when he was circumcised". You know the rest of the story: God visited Sarah as He had promised. Sarah conceived and bore Abraham a son in his old age, at the set time of which God had spoken to him, and Abraham was a hundred years old.

It was hearing God speak to him personally that produced that kind of faith or confidence toward God. Earlier in the book I expressed the difference between the (Logos & Rhema), which are New Testament or Greek definitions. Noah and Abraham are Old Testament individuals. I looked at the Hebrew definition for "word" in the Old Testament and found that "Dabar" expressed the same meaning as the "Logos" and Imrah or Emrah" expressed the same meaning for "Rhema". I believe that's why the Holy Spirit referenced them in the New Testament. This indicates there's no difference, when God speak to an individual, and the individual obeys and see the results: It produces Unshakable faith. I could show you many more Phenomenon's of Faith and they are all based on God Speaking to the individual and not the Individual approaching God with a book of confessions or positive thinking.

The Spirit of God is still speaking to his people today. When you prepare yourself to hear the Spirit of God speak to you: by studying to show yourself approved unto Him. Purifying the soul through obeying the truth unto unfeigned love of the Brethren, which means to have a genuine love for the Brethren! Be transformed by the renewing of the mind. Then take control of your thoughts by thinking on whatsoever things that are true, honest, just, pure, lovely and of a good report. Submit yourself to God and resist the demands of the flesh. Instead of bringing forth corruption, you will bring forth that what is good and acceptable, and perfect will of God. So walk as Children of light to bring forth fruit unto Eternal Life by putting on the Breastplate of Faith and Love and for a Helmet: THE HOPE OF SALVATION. HALLELUJAH AND AMEN!!!